Lift off!

Written by Gemma Bagnall
Illustrated by Eva Morales

It was Friday afternoon, and Miss Aman couldn't wait to share her box of stories. "What will you choose?" she asked.

Billy made a quick decision. "This looks like part of a rocket!" he said.

"You're right," replied Miss Aman, smiling.

At Billy's place, Billy, Bella-Rose and Tam began work on the rocket control panel.

As they cut and stuck, they thought about where they could go in their rocket.

4

Finally, the panel was nearly ready.

"One last thing," said Billy. "The steering wheel is essential!"

They headed to their special rocket.
After some jiggling, the panel lit up with a flash.

"We could zoom to the Moon!" said Tam.

"Or catch a shooting star!" said Bella-Rose.

"Let's visit Mars!" said Billy.

They held on tight as the rocket sprang into action.

"WE HAVE LIFT OFF!" they all shouted.

9

"That's the Moon!" cried Tam.

"A shooting star!" called Bella-Rose. "Let's catch it!"

"We must be close to Mars now," said Billy.

Just then, the control panel started beeping loudly and quickly.

"Watch out – asteroids!" shouted Bella-Rose, pointing at two huge space rocks. "They're heading right for us!" cried Tam.

"Not if I can help it!" said Billy, turning the steering wheel sharply to the left. With a jolt, the rocket shot sideways.

"Phew," said Tam. "That was close!"

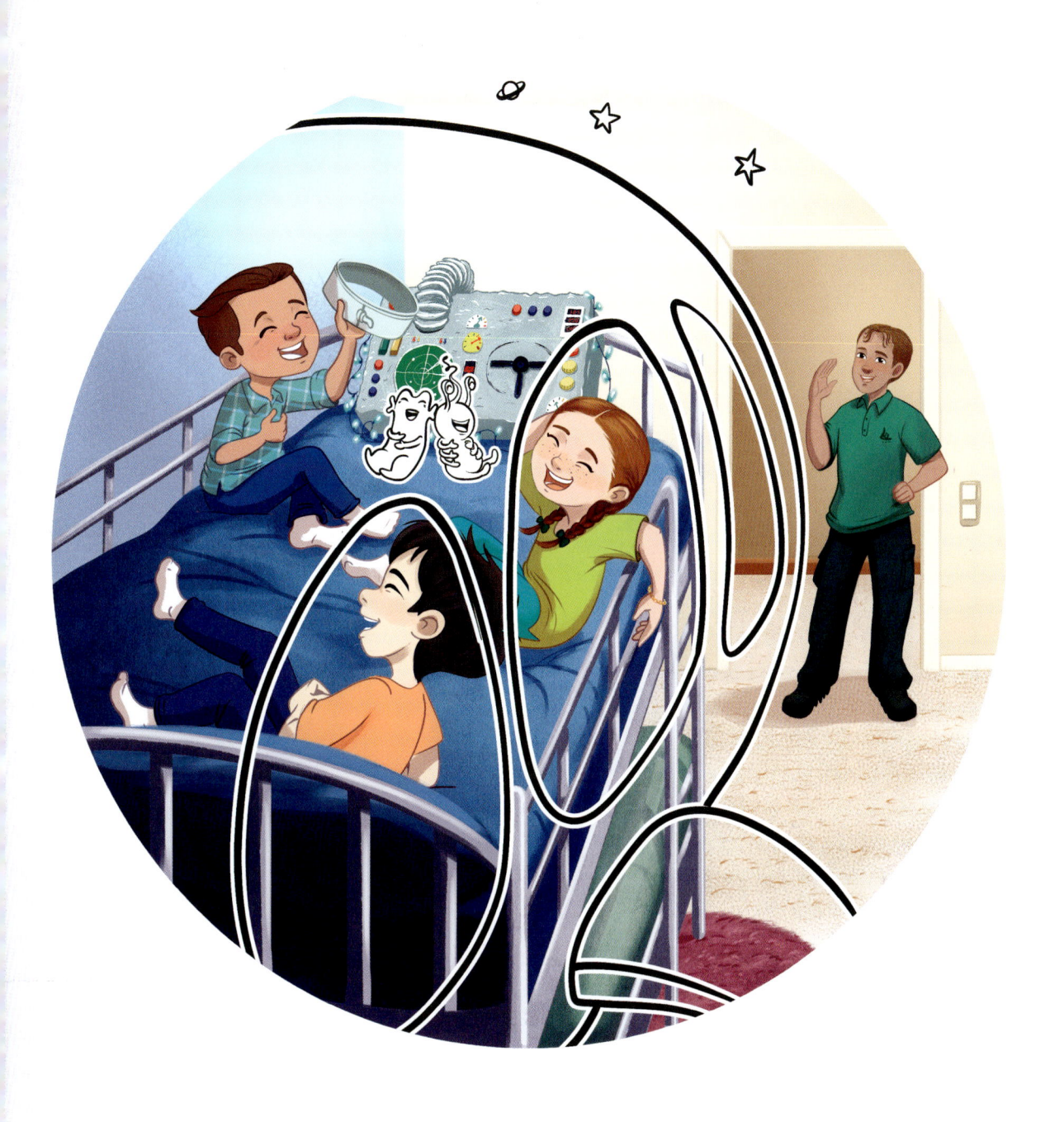

"Ground control to rocket crew," came the voice of Billy's brother from the hallway. "Time to turn that rocket around. Dinner's ready!"

"That was so much fun," said Bella-Rose, climbing down from the rocket.

"I can't wait to tell Miss Aman all about it," replied Tam.

"We didn't make it to Mars," said Billy, "but today's story was still out of this world!"